Sacred Desire

SECRETS TO KINDLING
PROFOUND PASSION

ROBERT E. WAGNER

Sacred Desire: Secrets to Kindling Profound Passion

Robert E. Wagner
Wild Sacredness, LLC
Ashland, Oregon
www.wildsacredness.com

©2016 Wild Sacredness, LLC

The following author and her publisher have generously granted permission to include excerpts on pages 11 and 12 from the following: ©Watkins Media Limited. From *Pure Kama Sutra* by Nicole Bailey (Watkins, London, 2005).

ISBN: 978-0-9863114-4-4

Second Edition

Printed in the United States of America
10 9 8 7 6 5 4 3 2

For the men and women who consciously choose to invite a profound level of surrender, intimacy and ecstasy into their loving relationships.

"WHEN LOVE IS ACCOMPANIED BY DEEP
INTIMACY, IT RAISES US TO THE HIGHEST
LEVEL OF HUMAN EXPERIENCE. IN THIS
EXALTED SPACE, WE CAN SURRENDER OUR
EGOS, BECOME VULNERABLE AND KNOW
LEVELS OF JOY AND WELL-BEING UNIQUE
AMONG LIFE EXPERIENCES. WE ATTAIN A
GLIMPSE OF THE RAPTURE THAT CAN BE
OURS. BOUNDARIES ARE BLURRED, THERE
ARE NO LIMITATIONS AND WE REJOICE
IN UNION. WE BECOME ONE AND, AT THE
SAME TIME, BOTH."

~ LEO BUSCAGLIA

Introduction

EVER WONDERED—when first falling in love or dreaming about the perfect relationship—just how deeply passionate the connection between two people can be?

An immersion into Sacred Desire reveals that we contain within us an unlimited reservoir of erotic energy and sensual pleasure. At Wild Sacredness, we recognize the importance of being fully present in order to tap into this reservoir and experience its many gifts. The initial tools of Sacred Desire presented in this booklet are just a taste—three foundational practices we use to open up to the vast vistas offered by Wild Sacredness. They offer a glimpse, letting you explore how conscious presence can uplift the simplest glance or touch into a truly sacred experience of bliss. Once you've completed this booklet, we invite you to explore the depths of Sacred Desire by visiting our website, **www.wildsacredness.com**. There you'll find many delightful offerings, some of them described below:

You'll begin with the techniques of Wild Intimacy, which invite Divine Energy into your relationship, creating channels for passion, bliss, and sexual pleasure to flow. These techniques will begin to soften obstacles that may be inhibiting the flow of your sexual energy, or Shakti. These enjoyable practices will reconnect you with your sexual innocence and set the stage for conscious lovemaking.

Going deeper into Tantra's mysteries, you'll learn to comfortably deepen and extend your lovemaking, as it becomes a conscious meditation, a merging of physical, emotional, and spiritual energies. Practicing Sacred Honoring, Conscious Presence, Breath, Sound, Movement and Visualization techniques, and Mudras, you'll learn how to affect energy on a very subtle level. Ejaculation Control for Men and Awakening Female Ejaculation for Women are practices that extend the blissful moments in lovemaking. Finally, the profound healing technique of Sacred Spot Massage for both men and women allows for release of deep-seated traumas or negative associations that may inhibit your full experience of pleasure during lovemaking.

Finally, you'll have the opportunity to experience and to learn how to give a Sacred Tantric Awakening session: a safe, blissful journey that opens you to the sheer delight and healing power of Tantra. Enjoy the blissful experience of receiving a session or two for yourself, then you can be trained to give one of these sessions to your partner. Your senses will be nourished and enlivened with mesmerizing music, aromatherapy, warmed natural massage oils and lotions, and soft candlelight. When you then learn how to give this very special gift of spirit and body, you'll become not only a sublime lover but also a profound healer for your lover.

THE EXERCISES

"WHEN EYE CONTACT BETWEEN TWO
PEOPLE IS INITIATED AND MAINTAINED,
AN INVISIBLE ENERGETIC CIRCUIT
IS ESTABLISHED BETWEEN THE TWO
PARTICIPANTS, DISSOLVING THE
BARRIERS THAT ORDINARILY SEPARATE
THEM FROM EACH OTHER, DRAWING
THEM EVER CLOSER INTO A SHARED
AWARENESS OF UNION."

~ WILL JOHNSON

Soul Gazing

IT'S BEEN SAID THAT THE EYES ARE THE "WINDOWS TO THE SOUL." To truly see and be seen by another is a profound experience. This simple practice of maintaining eye contact with your loved one is one of the most powerful ways to tune in to the sacred connection between you. Soul gazing opens you up to a profound level of intimacy, where you can perceive the deeper, divine essence of your partner, as well as the divine connection that gently and lovingly binds you as a couple.

You'll settle into the practice as if slipping into a soft meditation; as you focus on your lover's eyes, you're naturally drawn into a deeper connection and begin to perceive not just the forms but the formless presence and energy there. It's like melting into the other's soul. In this moment of oneness—where two souls are mirroring one another—you can actually exchange information and send feelings of love to your partner through your eyes.

Soul gazing is a spiritual as well as a physical exercise. It's a receptive process, where you allow the experience to flow spontaneously. As you begin soul gazing, remember that this is not about staring, but rather softly gazing into your partner's eyes and feeling the energy coming from them.

As with all the exercises and tools offered by Wild Sacredness, being fully present is the key to successful, fulfilling results. Before you begin this practice, settle into yourself quietly and set the intention to bring all of yourself to the moment. You might say something like, "I now let go of all distractions, all effort, all focus on any outcome, and simply open myself to being fully present." Your experience will be greatly enhanced by bringing the power of your PRESENCE to this activity.

~ Sit comfortably across from one another and close your eyes. Begin to synchronize your breathing. When you are ready, open your eyes and begin to look into your lover's eyes. It's easier to look into one eye than both, so focus on your partner's left eye—the left is said to be more receptive.

~ Relax into the gaze, but stay focused. You don't need to strain. If you feel like smiling, go ahead, and then comfortably let the smile fade. It's fine to blink when you need to.

~ Still your mind as you gaze, letting go of background "noise" as you focus completely on your partner's presence. Let yourself bond through gazing deeply into his or her eyes, becoming aware of the divine nature underlying the physical form. Feel free to give and receive love through your eyes, repeating "I love you" in your mind or sending intentions of love.

~ If you feel self-conscious or uncomfortable during this exercise, just acknowledge those feelings and then let them fade away. If you feel your attention slipping, bring your awareness back to your breath and the present moment. Don't speak during soul gazing—it's a time for non-verbal connection.

~ Soul gazing can be a powerful experience that can bring up a variety of emotions, including peacefulness and bliss or sadness and tears. You may even experience body sensations, such as twitching or chills. As you surrender to what arises, your experience will become deeper and richer. If strong emotions or sensations occur, such as a wave of grief or bodily shaking, feel into them and within a few minutes they should subside. If need be, feel free to close your eyes to center and regain your composure.

~ To heighten the experience of soul gazing, try placing your right hand on the other's heart, and your left hand on your own heart. Notice the transfer of energy.

~ Soul gazing can also be practiced solo, sitting facing a mirror. Follow the same guidelines as above, first seeing little things about yourself and eventually gazing into your left eye for as long as you can. This practice helps you know yourself more deeply and become comfortable with intimacy.

~ Another valuable time to practice soul gazing is while lying next to each other. It can easily be performed in the morning before starting the day, or at night before ending the day. Couples find that these intimate moments foster a closeness that remains even when they're not together.

~ When you finish the session, give one another a full-body embrace. This honors the divinity you've discovered in one another through the soul gazing exercise.

Soul gazing is a beautiful way to honor one another and the relationship that you share. We invite you to practice this simple ritual daily, even if only for a few minutes. It's a valuable tool for engaging your divinity, drinking in that sweet celestial connection that will bring passion and ecstasy to your lovemaking. If incorporated into your day, soul gazing will keep the loving energy flowing and bring you the blissful intimacy you both desire.

Soul gazing can have a therapeutic effect as you continue the practice. The intense love that is generated loosens stagnant energy and limiting beliefs or wounds, which are gently healed and released. As you open up to more feelings, a blissful awareness of sacred love begins to grow. Then the "real" relationship can begin.

"BE IN YOUR FINGERS AND HANDS AS IF YOUR WHOLE BEING, YOUR WHOLE SOUL, IS THERE."

~ OSHO

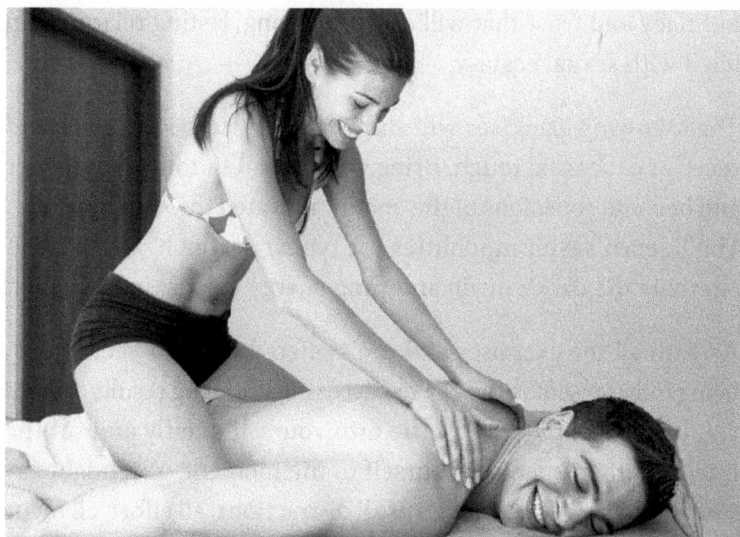

Sensual Touch

OUR BODIES ARE SACRED VESSELS, temples of the Divine Spirit dwelling within us. They enjoy being touched. Not only does touch nourish our senses, hearts and minds; it also connects us to the world around us. As children, we're very attuned to our bodies and how touch can bring pleasure, but as adults that spontaneous physical connection can be lost. Even in sexual activity our body awareness may be dulled, due to stress and lovemaking that has become too routine.

But waiting inside you is a reservoir of unlimited sexual energy and bliss. Exploring your own body through self-touch and self-pleasuring will help you rediscover your own erotic pleasure points, which you can then share with your partner. As you exchange information about how you both like to be touched, you're learning valuable tools for lovemaking, while building intimacy and trust that will create a strong, lasting relationship filled with sexual ecstasy.

The following exercises will show you how to be the giver and receiver of sensual touch. Bring your full attention to your lover and become conscious of the energy activated through touching. You'll learn seven modalities (or types) of touch, and how to alternate the dance of yin and yang energy for maximum effect.

As with all the exercises and tools offered by Wild Sacredness, being fully present is the key to successful, fulfilling results. Before you begin this practice, settle into yourself quietly and set the intention to bring all of yourself to the moment. You might say something like, "I now let go of all distractions, all effort, all focus on any outcome, and simply open myself to being fully present." Your experience will be greatly enhanced by bringing the power of your PRESENCE to this activity.

~ After creating a warm, inviting space, decide which of you will be the giver (active) and which the receiver (receptive). When giving a sensual massage, we recommend using a quality massage oil. Begin to explore your partner's body in a loving, respectful and nonsexual way, as if discovering it for the first time. Notice the feelings of skin, the texture of hair, the contours of muscle and bone that you encounter.

~ Pay attention to your hands during sensual massage. Feel the heart energy moving through them with your touch—and focus on sending love, compassion and nurturing to your partner. Feel free to use your fingers and fingernails, knuckles and elbows, and the heel and edge of your hand as you massage, all the while being aware of giving and receiving love through this intimate exchange.

~ Be creative—try using your forearms and feet to produce varying pressure on your partner's body. Teeth and tongue are useful to stroke and caress. Try licking your lover's neck, then blowing on it. Try touching with different materials such as feathers, paintbrushes or ice cubes. Ear lobes, palms and faces are also very sensitive to massage.

~ Vary your touch—there are seven levels of pressure (light to deep) and motion (slow to fast) you can apply. Keep changing your movements so that no area becomes numb to a repeated style of touch.

~ Use your conscious awareness to bring more energy into your massage. Imagine energy growing into your lover's body through your fingers, and feel the energy circuit moving from your right hand, through your partner, into your left hand.

~ Make contact with all the chakra points, on the front and back. Be aware of the mind/body connection, so that your partner will experience maximum pleasure.

~ Experiment with the following modalities, based on the work of Charles Muir, Source School of Tantra:

1. Static touch (non-moving)

2. Moving touch: short and long strokes, circles, spirals, sideways strokes, and triangles

3. Scratching or grazing with teeth

4. Squeezing, kneading and pinching

5. Tapping/slapping

6. Vibrating/shaking

7. Nyasa – this refers to a sacred ritual that includes touching each of the seven chakras while visualizing a Yantra (geometric shape of the corresponding chakra) and reciting a Bija mantra (vibratory tone of the corresponding chakra).

~ Explore the 'Yin' and 'Yang' as expressed in each modality. Yin is characterized as slow, soft, diffuse, cold, wet and tranquil. It is generally associated with the feminine, birth and generation, and with night. Yang is characterized as hard, fast, solid, dry, focused, hot, and aggressive. It is associated with masculinity and daytime. Use both expressions in your touch, as more healing and energy are produced when a yin stroke is followed by a yang stroke, and vice-versa.

Rediscovering the rich mysteries contained in our bodies is the point of sensual touch. As you learn where your pleasure comes from, and how to activate that pleasure in your partner, the treasure chest of sexual ecstasy and sacred love is opened.

After spending up to an hour exploring your partner's body with these exercises, it's time to switch roles—now you'll be the receiver and give your partner the opportunity to lavish the sweet attention on you! After you're done, take time to discuss your experiences with each other. You'll learn a lot about how your partner takes in pleasure. Practicing sensual touch in this lively, conscious and open-hearted way will continue to open new doors in your lovemaking and growing intimacy.

"TWAS NOT MY LIPS YOU KISSED, BUT MY SOUL."

~ JUDY GARLAND

Erotic Kissing

EROTIC KISSING CAN RANGE FROM AN EXTREMELY SUBTLE caress to a passionate embrace. Whether kissing is soft and tender or full of steamy passion, a powerful circuit of energy is created—where even the slightest touch can cause your partner to surrender in your arms.

Remember the sensual thrill of kissing your first boyfriend or girlfriend? That delicious, intimate arousal is often missing in long-term relationships, but it can be brought back with a little playfulness and creativity.

Erotic kissing is one of the pillars of Sacred Desire, a lush beginning to lovemaking. However, it can also stand on its own as a deep bond between two people. In fact, vital essences and energies are exchanged in erotic kissing, and saliva is believed to have a harmonizing effect on the Yin and Yang influences within a couple. The more you can melt into a full, deeply passionate kiss, the more romantic intimacy you'll experience.

As with all the exercises and tools offered by Wild Sacredness, being fully present is the key to successful, fulfilling results. Before you begin this practice, settle into yourself quietly and set the intention to bring all of yourself to the moment. You might say something like, "I now let go of all distractions, all effort, all focus on any outcome, and simply open myself to being fully present." Your experience will be greatly enhanced by bringing the power of your PRESENCE to this activity.

~ Sit next to each other on the couch, or if you prefer, in the Tantric 'Yab Yum' position:

The male partner sits cross-legged, comfortably so his knees don't feel stressed or the leg muscles too tight. The female partner then sits on top of him so they are facing one another. The woman on top places her thighs on either side of the man's waist and wraps her legs around him in a close grip— so the two are comfortably connected. This will allow you to comfortably relax and focus your attention on the sweet task at hand. (Please note: The words 'male' and 'female' have been used for verbal clarity; same-sex couples are free to adapt the position allowing for maximum comfort.)

~ As with the Sensual Touch exercise, decide which of you will be the giver (active) and which will be the receiver (receptive). Then approach your lover and begin to explore his or her lips and mouth in a playful way.

~ Gently kiss your partner's mouth, first the upper lip and then the lower lip. After a while let your tongue softly caress their moist lips.

~ Allow your mouths and tongues to engage in a dance, retreating and advancing, darting and circling.

~ Feel your physical and emotional boundaries start to dissolve as you linger in the sumptuous warmth of your joined lips, letting go of yourselves in a deep erotic kiss.

~ Employ these various modalities in your kissing: stillness, sucking, blowing, tonguing, and even gentle biting.

~ Incorporate expressions of both Yin and Yang into your kissing. Yin is related to: light pressure, slow speed, softness, shallow touch, lower lip. Yang is related to: hard pressure, fast speed, firmness, deep touch, upper lip.

Alternate roles of giver (yang) and receiver (yin). Kiss the lips one at a time, then together. Remember to keep your lips and facial muscles relaxed and soft during your kissing.

*Try this exercise in Conscious Kissing:**

~ Both of you promise to do nothing but kiss each other—for as long as possible. Stand close to your lover with your eyes closed and your lips almost touching. Breathe softly in and out so that your breath brushes the other's lips. Now gently graze the surface of his or her lips with yours before drawing your lover's lower lip into your mouth and caressing it with your lips and tongue (try experimenting with your teeth too). Explore the inside of your lover's mouth—as your kisses become more intimate, allow yourself to get carried away by them.

~ Don't think about what you're going to do next or whether or not kissing will lead to sex—just kiss for the sake of kissing. If your mind wanders, bring your attention back to the sensations in your body. Allow your senses to open up so that you really begin to relish the taste, smell and feel of your lover's lips and tongue against yours. Lose yourself in the act of kissing—the more absorbed you become in the experience, the more deeply connected you will become to your lover.

*From *Pure Kama Sutra* by Nicole Bailey

Recommit yourself to the wonderful art of kissing. The erotic kiss offers a profoundly intimate sexual exchange between two lovers. It wakes up dormant passions, drawing out sensual responses from all parts of your body and rekindling your sacred sexual energy.

IF YOU'VE FOUND THE INFORMATION in this booklet helpful and inspiring, then we invite you to learn more at: **www. wildsacredness.com**. Click on the "Sacred Desire" offering to learn more about experiencing the flow of passion–physical, emotional, and spiritual–in your intimate relationships. Pleasure and mutual fulfillment are the natural birthright of everyone–so why not open the door?

If these exercises have sparked you to go deeper, give Robert a call at 541-201-3411 or email robert@wildsacredness.com. He offers a **FREE "Reignite the Passion in Your Relationship" session**—where you can share the results from the exercises one-on-one with a qualified instructor, and learn how the tools of Wild Sacredness will keep elevating your relationship to new heights of blissful rapture. Here's what the session will do for you:

1. Create a sense of clarity about the relationship you most desire.

2. Uncover the essential building blocks required to have the relationship of your dreams.

3. Reveal the #1 thing blocking you from having that relationship.

4. Identify the actions needed to manifest your passionate relationship.

5. Show you EXACTLY what to do next to create your dream relationship!

Robert also offers presentations and lively experiential workshops —in a safe, fun environment—to ignite passion and pleasure in relationships.

Wild Sacredness is dedicated to bringing forth the authentic, passionate essence within each of us, and nurturing that as we manifest our individual power and purpose, our capacity for deep, intimate relationships, and a dynamic, engaged relationship with our community.

ROBERT E. WAGNER
Founder and Director, Wild Sacredness

WILD SACREDNESS is the outgrowth of the inner and outer journeying Robert has been doing for most of his life. As an Eagle Scout and member of the Order of the Arrow, he spent his first time alone in the wilderness as a young teen. Soon after that, he began his practice of Transcendental Meditation and spent many years living and studying in a prominent spiritual community.

In 1996, Robert participated in his first vision quest; he has continued to use the quest as a tool for empowerment and self-awareness, going on a vision quest every year. The discovery of Tantra as a vehicle for profound healing and fulfillment fit perfectly into Robert's array of tools for embracing one's wild, sacred, sensual presence and sharing that with others. As a member of the Mankind New Warrior Project and creator of men's empowerment groups, he has honed skills as a personal development facilitator and community builder.

In addition to his qualifications as a professional wilderness guide, certified Tantra educator and group facilitator, Robert brings 35 years of success in the corporate world as a marketing executive and multi-craft technician. He is also the father of a daughter in her thirties.

A compassionate and gifted communicator, Robert approaches people with deep respect and intuitive wisdom. He has developed an uncommon ability to create a safe, sacred space supporting profound transformation for individuals, respectful of their unique personal paths and pace of growth.

For a full listing of Robert's credentials, visit
www.wildsacredness.com

The exercises contained within this booklet are an introduction to the full range of tools offered by Wild Sacredness to maximize pleasure, passion, and ecstasy in your intimate relationships. To appreciate the impact of the profound and far-reaching effects of Tantra, take a moment and read what men and women are saying about their experiences with the teachings of Sacred Desire.

"Tantra is about presence and holding sacred space, and recognizing divinity in every moment. It starts with yourself, and what you can bring to the other. I bring me to the we—and who is the me that I'm bringing? Tantra showed me a lot about myself, and how I can give that to my partner."

~ MATT – WILLIAMS, OR

"My husband and I feel we have more tools now to deepen our relationship. We've embarked on a journey down an entirely new path of intimacy due to this Tantric Awakening session, and we're excited about the potential. It was extremely transformational."

~ GABRIELLA – ASHLAND, OR

"A Sacred Tantric Awakening session feels like honey—so sweet and loving. It made me love being a woman and reminded me how divinely feminine I am."

~ KIM – CORTE MADERA, CA

"Tantra offers the tools to create healthy sexuality—a more expansive view than what most of us have grown up with. This knowledge doesn't belong just to the young, either. People often slip into old age as their sexual energy declines. As we learn to move our energy we're reminded how great it feels to look good, to feel attractive. It comes from inside, truly."

~ MARGARET – ASHLAND, OR

"Robert did a tremendous job with material that's very intimate and difficult for some people to address. Some old fears cropped up, and I was able to let them go. I feel amazingly lucky to have found an expert such as Robert—he's considerate, discreet, and very knowledgeable."

~ MARK – ASHLAND, OR

"My sessions with Robert have generated a whole new path of exploration that is very exciting and rewarding for me. The work brought together emotional, spiritual and sexual aspects of myself, merging them into one harmonious whole - while healing some past trauma. I love this blend of merging sexuality with spirituality in lovemaking! At 54, this feels like a new beginning!"

~ FRANCE – MEDFORD, OR

"When my husband began my Tantric Awakening session, after training with Robert, I was skeptical and nervous because of previous sexual wounding. Within a few minutes, it felt like we had entered another dimension. I relaxed and began to feel some softening of the blocks I had from prior sexual trauma. My husband lovingly talked me through it, assuring me with his touch. Now I know, from just one session with my husband, that anything can be healed."

~ LUCINDA – ASHLAND, OR

"Robert, thank you again for the tremendous gift of your presence! I am still in awe of my healing experience and the safe and loving space you held for me."

~ KERRY – SAN FRANCISCO, CA

"I think everyone could benefit from Tantra. It reawakens your self-love, which is important for any relationship to be successful, as well as teaching new skills to bring that love tangibly and blissfully to your partner."

~ ROBIN – WILLIAMS, OR

"My friends all noticed something different about me after a Tantric Awakening session – more vitality and aliveness. Unlocking sexual energy creates such a powerful glow! My partner and I are more present, more passionate and more in love now than when we first met years ago!"

~ SARAH – MEDFORD, OR

Other books by Robert E. Wagner in the Wild Sacredness Series, available at www.amazon.com (print or Kindle eBook format):

WILDNESS WITHIN: Experience the Power of Your Authentic Self
A journey of exploration into your most prized possession—your unique, wonderful self and the many gifts you have to offer.

EMBRACING COMMUNITY: Living an Inspired Life
Takes you on one of the most intimate of all adventures—finding the purpose for your life and living it, in vibrant engagement with people you care about.

08132016

www.ingramcontent.com/pod-product-compliance
Lightning Source LLC
Chambersburg PA
CBHW060550030426
42337CB00021B/4513